The Prisoner of Zenda

Anthony Hope

Text adaptation by Diane Mowat
Illustrated by Katy Jackson

Original Bookworms Series Editor:
Jennifer Bassett

OXFORD
UNIVERSITY PRES

Activities

Before reading

Rudolf Rassendyll is a young, rich Englishman. But his family is related to the royal family of Ruritania, and he has the dark red hair and the long straight nose of an Elphberg. Rudolf decides to visit Ruritania for the coronation of the new king. He arrives in the town of Zenda and goes for a quiet walk in the forest. By the next morning he is in the middle of adventures beyond his wildest dreams. With his new friends Captain Sapt and Fritz von Tarlenheim, he is making plans to rescue the King, who is a prisoner in the Castle of Zenda. Soon he is fighting the King's enemies, Black Michael the Duke and Rupert of Hentzau.

1 **Read the introduction to the story. Then answer these questions about Rudolf Rassendyll.**

   Who does Rudolf Rassendyll . . .

   1 look like?   _____

   2 make friends with? _____

   3 try to rescue?   _____

   4 fight against?   _____

2 **What do you think will happen in the story? Choose words to complete the passage.**

   The story happens in Ruritania, which *is / is not* a real place, and is an *adventure / animal* story. There will be lots of *accidents / fighting* in the Castle of Zenda, and in the end the King's *enemies / friends* will *rescue / kill* him. The story will end *happily / sadly* for the King, and Rudolf Rassendyll will *leave / stay in* Ruritania.

Chapter 1 **The Rassendylls – and the Elphbergs**

'When are you going to do something useful, Rudolf?' my brother's wife asked. She looked at me crossly over the breakfast table.

'But why should I do anything, Rose?' I answered, calmly eating my egg. 'I've got enough money for the things I want, and my brother, Robert, is a lord – Lord Burlesdon. I'm very happy.'

'You're twenty-nine, and you've done nothing.'

'It's true. We Rassendylls are a rich and famous family, and we don't need to do anything.'

This made Rose angry. 'Rich and famous families sometimes behave worse than less important families,' she said.

crossly angrily

lord a title for a nobleman (less important than a duke)

behave to do things well or badly

When I heard this, I touched my dark red hair.

'I'm so pleased that Robert's hair is black!' she cried.

Just then my brother, Robert, came in. When he looked at Rose, he could see that there was something wrong.

'What's the matter, my dear?' he said.

'Oh, she's angry because I never do anything useful, and because I've got red hair,' I said.

'Well, I know he can't do much about his hair, or his nose ...' Rose began.

'No, the nose and the hair are in the family,' my brother agreed. 'And Rudolf has both of them.'

Maybe I should stop for a moment and explain that the Rassendylls are descendants of Prince Rudolf of Ruritania, of the Elphberg family. Prince Rudolf had blue eyes, an unusually long straight nose and a lot of dark red hair. He was tall and very good-looking, but he was also a scoundrel. So, for many generations the Rassendylls have preferred to forget they were once closely related to the Elphbergs.

But because my hair was red and I had the Elphberg nose, Rose worried about me. In the end, I promised to get a job in six months' time. This gave me six free months to enjoy myself first.

And an idea came to me — I would visit Ruritania. None of my family had ever been there. I saw in the newspaper that, in three weeks, the new young King, Rudolf the Fifth, would have his coronation. It would be an interesting time to visit the country.

I knew my family would not like me to go, so I told them I was going walking in Austria.

Chapter 2 **The colour of men's hair**

On the way to Ruritania I decided to spend a night in Paris with a friend. The next morning he came with me to the station, and as we waited for the train we watched the crowds. We saw a tall, dark, very fashionable lady, and my friend told me who she was.

'That's Madame Antoinette de Mauban. She's travelling on the same train as you. She's a friend of Duke Michael of Strelsau. And he, as you know, is the half-brother of the new King of Ruritania. Although he's only the second son and will never be king himself, he's still an important man and very popular with many Ruritanians.'

I did not speak to the lady during the journey, and when we arrived in Ruritania I left the train at Zenda, a small

fashionable
popular

Duke a title for
an important
nobleman

town outside the capital. But I saw that Madame de Mauban went on to Strelsau, the capital.

I was welcomed very kindly at my hotel. It belonged to an old lady and her daughter. From them I learned that the coronation was to be on the day after next, and not in three weeks.

The old lady was more interested in Duke Michael of Strelsau than in the new King. The Castle of Zenda and all the land around it belonged to the Duke, but the old lady said, 'Duke Michael should be king. He spends all his time with us. Every Ruritanian knows him, but we never see the new King.'

But her daughter cried, 'Oh no, I hate Black Michael. I want a red Elphberg — and the King, our friend Johann says, is very red. Johann works for the Duke and he's seen the King. In fact, the King's staying just outside Zenda now,' she added. 'He's resting at the Duke's hunting lodge in the forest before going on to Strelsau on Wednesday for his coronation. The Duke's already in Strelsau, getting everything ready.'

'Are they friends?' I asked.

'Friends who want the same place and the same wife,' the girl replied. 'The Duke wants to marry his cousin, Princess Flavia, but people say she's going to be King Rudolf's wife and become the Queen.'

Just then their friend, Johann, entered the room.

'We have a visitor, Johann,' the girl's mother said, and Johann turned towards me. But when he saw me, he stepped back, with a look of surprise on his face.

'What's the matter, Johann?' the daughter asked.

'Good evening, sir,' Johann said, still looking at me. He did not seem to like what he saw.

capital the main city of a country

belong to someone to be someone's thing, to be owned

lodge a house where people stay in the country

The girl began to laugh. 'It's the colour of your hair, sir,' she explained. 'We don't often see that colour here. It's the Elphberg red – not Johann's favourite colour.'

*   *   *

The next day I decided to walk through the forest for a few miles and take the train to Strelsau from a little station along the road. I sent my luggage on the train and after lunch I started out on foot. First, I wanted to see the Castle of Zenda and in half an hour I had climbed the hill to it. There were two buildings – the old one, with a moat around it, and the new, modern building. Duke Michael could have friends to stay with him in the new castle, but he could go into the old castle when he wanted to be alone. The water in the moat was deep, and if he pulled up the drawbridge over the moat, no one could get to him.

I stayed there for some time and looked at the castle, and then I walked on through the forest for about an hour.

forest a place with a lot of trees

moat a deep wide ditch around a castle, filled with water

drawbridge a bridge across the moat of a castle that can be pulled up to stop people crossing

Good heavens! an expression to show great surprise

It was beautiful and I sat down to enjoy it. Before I knew what had happened, I was asleep.

Suddenly I heard a voice say, 'Good heavens! He looks just like the King!'

When I opened my eyes, there were two men in front of me. One of them came nearer.

'May I ask your name?' he said.

'Well, why don't you tell me your names first?' I replied.

The younger of the two men said, 'This is Captain Sapt, and I am Fritz von Tarlenheim. We work for the King of Ruritania.'

'And I am Rudolf Rassendyll,' I answered, 'a traveller from England. My brother is Lord Burlesdon.'

Just then a voice called out from the trees behind us. 'Fritz! Fritz! Where are you?'

'It's the King!' Fritz said, and Sapt laughed.

Then a young man jumped out from behind a tree. I gave a cry, and when he saw me he stepped back in

sudden surprise. The King of Ruritania looked just like Rudolf Rassendyll, and Rudolf Rassendyll looked just like the King!

For a moment the King said nothing, but then he asked, 'Captain ... Fritz ... who is this?'

Sapt went to the King and spoke quietly in his ear. The King's surprise changed slowly to an amused smile, then suddenly he began to laugh loudly. 'So, we must be cousins! Welcome to my country, cousin!' he cried. 'Where are you travelling to?'

'To Strelsau, sir – to the coronation.'

The King looked at his friends, and for a moment he was serious. But then he started to laugh again. 'Wait until brother Michael sees that there are two of us!' he cried.

'Maybe it isn't a very good idea for Mr Rassendyll to go to Strelsau,' Fritz said, worried, and Sapt agreed with him.

'Oh, we'll think about the coronation tomorrow,' the King said. 'Come, cousin!'

We returned to the Duke's lodge in the forest, where we had an excellent dinner.

After we had finished eating, old Josef, the King's servant, came in. He put down a plate in front of the King and said, 'Duke Michael offers you this cake on the day before your coronation.'

'Then we must thank Black Michael!' the King cried. 'Well, I'm not scared of his food!'

And he ate all that was on the plate.

Then Sapt said, 'It's late. Let's go to bed. Tomorrow is an important day.'

Soon after, we were all asleep.

servant someone who is paid to work in another person's house

Activities

1 Who do these sentences describe? Write the names.

Duke Michael   Rudolf Rassendyll   Antoinette de Mauban

Prince Rudolf   King Rudolf

1 He was tall and very good-looking but he was also a scoundrel.

_____Prince Rudolf_____

2 'She's travelling on the same train as you.'

_____

3 'He's only the second son and will never be king himself.'

_____

4 'Good heavens! He looks just like the King.'

_____

5 'Friends who want the same place and the same wife.'

_____ and _____

2 Who said this? Write the names.

Josef   Robert   Rose   King   Rudolf Rassendyll   daughter

1 'I'm so pleased that Robert's hair is black!' said _____Rose_____.

2 'No, the nose and the hair are in the family,' agreed _____.

3 'I hate Black Michael!' cried the _____.

4 'I am a traveller from England,' said _____.

5 'So, we must be cousins!' laughed the _____.

6 'Duke Michael offers you this cake,' said _____.

3 Correct the underlined words in these sentences.

1 'When are you going to do something <u>useless</u>, Rudolf?'   *useful*

2 Prince Rudolf had blue eyes, a long straight nose and <u>dart</u> red hair. _____

3 Because my hair was red and I had the Elphberg nose, Rose <u>worked</u> about me.

   _____

4 As we waited for the <u>trail</u> we watched the crowds. _____

5 'Although he's only the second son and will never be king himself, he's still an impossible <u>man</u>.' _____

6 'It's the Elphberg red – not Johann's favourite <u>collar</u>.' _____

7 Duke Michael went into the old castle when he wanted to be <u>along</u>.

   _____

8 We returned to the Duke's house, where we had an excellent <u>winner</u>.

   _____

4 Are these sentences true (T) or false (F)?

1 Rudolf Rassendyll is sad because he doesn't have a job.   F

2 Rudolf is interested in the new King of Ruritania.   ☐

3 The new King is Duke Michael's father.   ☐

4 The Castle of Zenda belongs to Duke Michael.   ☐

5 Johann and the old lady want Duke Michael to be king.   ☐

6 Rudolf meets the new King in the Castle of Zenda.   ☐

7 The King invites Rudolf to have dinner with him in the Duke's house.   ☐

8 The King and Black Michael like each other very much.   ☐

Chapter 3 **The King goes to his coronation**

When I woke up, Sapt and Fritz were standing next to my bed. 'Come with us, quickly,' said Fritz.

We went downstairs and there was the King, still in his clothes, lying on the floor. When Sapt pushed him with his hand, he did not move.

'We've been trying to wake him for half an hour,' said Fritz. 'But he's sleeping like a dead man.'

The three of us looked at each other.

'Was there something in that cake?' I asked.

'I don't know,' Sapt said, 'but if he doesn't get to his coronation today, there'll never be a coronation for him. All Ruritania is waiting for him in Strelsau and Black Michael with half the army, too. We can't tell them that the King can't wake up to go to his own coronation!'

'Tell me, do you think somebody put something in that cake?' I asked.

'It was Black Michael!' Fritz replied. 'We all know he wants to be King himself.'

For a moment or two we were all silent, and then Sapt looked at me and said, 'You must go to Strelsau and take his place!'

I looked at him. 'You're crazy, man! How can I do that? The King …'

'It's dangerous, I know,' said Sapt. 'But it's our only chance. If you don't go, Black Michael will be King and the real King will be dead or a prisoner.'

How could I say no? It took me two minutes to decide. 'I'll go!' I said.

'Well done, boy!' cried Sapt. He went on quickly and quietly. 'After the coronation they'll take us to the palace

army a large number of people who fight for their country

take someone's place to go instead of another person

real not false

prisoner a person who is caught and must stay in prison

for the night. When we're alone, you and I will leave and ride back here to fetch the King. He'll be all right by then. I'll take him back to Strelsau and you must get out of the country as fast as you can.'

'But what about the soldiers?' Fritz asked. 'They're Duke Michael's men, and they're coming to take the King back to Strelsau for the coronation.'

'We'll go before the soldiers get here,' Sapt said, 'and we'll hide the King.'

He lifted the King up from the floor and we opened the door. An old woman, Johann's mother, was standing there. She turned, without a word, and went back to the kitchen.

soldier a person in an army

hide (*past* **hid**) to go where people can't see you

lock to close with
a key

underground
below the ground,
under a house

mistake
something that is
wrong

'Did she hear?' Fritz asked.

'Don't worry. I'll make sure she can't talk,' Sapt said, and he carried the King away.

When he returned, he told us that he had locked the old woman in a room underground. The King and Josef were hidden in another room underground. 'Josef will take care of the King and tell him everything when he wakes up. Come,' he went on, 'there's no time to lose. It's already six o'clock.'

Soon I was dressed in the King's clothes, the horses were ready and we were on our way. As we rode through the forest, Sapt told me everything that he could about my life, my family, my friends, and the things I liked or did not like. He told me what to do when we got there, and how to speak to different people. He was a good teacher, and I listened hard. One mistake could be death for all three of us.

It was eight o'clock when we arrived at the station and got on the train, and by half-past nine we were in Strelsau.

And when King Rudolf the Fifth stepped out of the train, the people shouted, 'Long live the King!' Old Sapt smiled, 'Long live them both,' he said quietly.

'I only hope we are all alive tonight!'

Chapter 4 **My adventures begin**

As we made our way to the palace, I began to feel that I really was the King of Ruritania, with Marshal Strakencz, the head of the army, on my right and old Sapt on my left. I could see that Strelsau was really two towns – the Old Town and the New Town. The people of the Old Town, who were poor, wanted Duke Michael to be their King, but the people of the New Town wanted King Rudolf.

We went through the New Town first, and it was bright and colourful, with the ladies' dresses and the red roses of the Elphbergs. The people shouted for their King as we passed through the streets. But when we came to the Old Town, the Marshal and Sapt moved nearer to my horse, and I could see that they were worried about me.

'Stay back!' I called. 'I'll show my people that I'm not scared of them.' Some of the crowd were pleased when they heard this, but most of them watched me in silence.

Finally, we reached the great town hall of Strelsau. I remember very little of the coronation – only two faces. One was a woman with red hair, the Princess Flavia. The

Marshal a very important army officer

bright full of light, colourful

town hall the building in a town where important people work

other was the face of a man with black hair and dark, deep eyes – Black Michael. When he saw me, his face turned white. Clearly, he was surprised and very unhappy to see me.

The coronation seemed to last for hours, but I said and did all the right things. At last it was over, and I was now the King of Ruritania!

'I wonder what the real King is doing now,' I thought.

*   *   *

The royal dinner went on for a long time, but at last Fritz, Sapt and I were alone in the King's dressing room.

'You did well,' Fritz said, 'but, Rassendyll, be careful! Black Michael looked blacker than ever today.'

'Come on,' Sapt cried. 'We must leave for Zenda at once, to find the King! If we're caught, we'll all be killed! Black Michael has had a letter from Zenda, so perhaps he knows already. Don't unlock the door, Fritz, while we're away, or you'll be a dead man. Say the King must be left alone to rest. Now, come on. The horses are ready.'

Fritz and I shook hands, then I covered my red hair and most of my face. Sapt and I left the room by a secret door, and we found ourselves outside, at the back of the palace gardens. A man was waiting there with two horses.

Soon we left the town behind us and we were out in the country. We rode like the wind and by ten o'clock had come to the forest of Zenda.

Suddenly Sapt stopped. 'Listen!' he said quietly. 'Horses behind us! Quick! Get down!' The castle's to the left,' he continued. 'Our road's to the right.'

We hid in the thick trees, and we waited and watched. The men came nearer. It was Black Michael and another man. When they came to the two roads, they stopped.

'Which way?' the Duke asked.

'To the castle!' the other man cried. 'They'll know there what's been happening.'

The Duke waited for a moment. 'To Zenda then!' he cried finally, and the two men took the road to the left.

We waited for ten more minutes, and then we hurried on. When we arrived at the Duke's lodge in the forest, we ran to the underground rooms. The one where Sapt had locked up the old woman was empty. She had escaped! The other room was locked. Sapt's face was white with fear. Between us, we broke down the door and ran in. I found a light and looked around the room. The servant Josef was on the floor – dead! I held up the light and looked in every corner of the room.

'The King isn't here!' I said.

escape to get away

fear the feeling of being scared

Activities

1 **Rewrite these words from Chapters 3 and 4.**
Then complete each sentence with one word.

1 episrursd   s _surprised_

2 oaoicrtonn   c _____

3 lmsarah   m _____

4 loucnk   u _____

5 pedseca   e _____

6 loary   r _____

7 notstai   s _____

a 'We can't tell them that the King can't wake up to go to his _____ !'

b It was eight o'clock when we arrived at the _____ .

c Rudolf rode to the palace with the _____ on his right and Sapt on his left.

d Black Michael was _surprised_ and unhappy to see Rudolf.

e The _____ dinner went on for a long time.

f 'Don't _____ the door, Fritz, while we're away, or you'll be a dead man.'

g The underground room was empty. The old woman had _____ !

2 Match the two halves of the sentences.

1 The King was sleeping like a dead man . . . [f]

2 Sapt was worried that if the King didn't go to the coronation . . . [ ]

3 Rudolf agreed to . . . [ ]

4 Johann's mother listened to their plans . . . [ ]

5 On the way to Strelsau, Sapt told Rudolf . . . [ ]

6 At the coronation Black Michael's face turned white . . . [ ]

7 After the coronation Sapt told Rudolf . . . [ ]

8 When they went back to the Duke's lodge, they found that . . . [ ]

a he must go back with him and Fritz to Zenda to find the King.

b so Sapt locked her in a room underground.

c go to Strelsau and pretend to be the King.

d when he saw Rudolf.

e Josef was dead and the King had gone.

f and he couldn't go to the coronation.

g about the King and what he liked doing.

h Black Michael would be King.

3 What do you think happens next? Tick the boxes.

	Yes	No
1 Black Michael kills the King.	[ ]	[ ]
2 Rudolf goes back to Strelsau as the King.	[ ]	[ ]
3 Rudolf is hurt by a bullet.	[ ]	[ ]
4 Black Michael locks Fritz in a room.	[ ]	[ ]
5 Rudolf decides to tell the people he is not the real King.	[ ]	[ ]
6 Sapt finds out where the real King is.	[ ]	[ ]

Chapter 5 **His Majesty returns to Strelsau**

It was one o'clock in the morning. For a few minutes we said nothing. Then Sapt cried, 'The Duke's men have taken the King prisoner!'

'Then we must get back and wake everyone in Strelsau!' I cried. 'We must catch Black Michael before he kills the King.'

'Who knows where the King is now?' Sapt answered. Then suddenly he began to laugh. 'But we've given Black Michael a problem,' he said. 'Yes, my boy. We'll go back to Strelsau. The King will be in his palace in Strelsau again tomorrow.'

'No!' I cried.

'Yes!' Sapt answered. 'It's the only way to help him. Go back and take his place for him.'

'But the Duke knows …'

'Yes, but he can't speak, can he? What can he say? "This man isn't the King because I've taken the real King prisoner and murdered his servant." Can he say that?'

'But people will soon know I'm not the real King,' I said.

'Maybe, maybe not,' said Sapt. 'But we must have a King in Strelsau, or Michael will ride in tomorrow as the new King! Listen, boy, if you don't go back to Strelsau, they'll kill the King. And if you *do* go back, they *can't* kill the King. Because if they kill him, how can they ever say that you're not the real King? Don't you see?' he cried. 'It's a dangerous game, but it gives us a chance of winning.'

It was a wild, hopeless plan, but I was young. I would never have the chance of an adventure like this again. 'Sapt, I'll try it,' I said.

adventure
something very exciting that happens to you

'Good for you!' Sapt cried. 'But we must hurry! Look!' He pulled me over to the door. The moon was low now and there was not much light, but I could just see a small group of men on horses. They were Black Michael's men, probably coming to take the dead body of Josef away.

'We can't let them go without doing something,' I said, thinking of poor Josef.

'Right,' Sapt agreed. We ran out of the back of the house and quickly got onto our horses. Silently, we waited in the darkness, and then we galloped round the house, and straight into the group of men. Between us, we killed three of them, but a bullet hit my finger and it started to bleed.

gallop horses do this when they run fast

We rode hard all night and it was about eight or nine o'clock in the morning when we reached Strelsau. Luckily the streets were still empty. We arrived at the palace, went in, and got to the dressing room. When we opened the door, Fritz was asleep, but he woke immediately. When he saw me, he fell to the ground and cried, 'Your Majesty! You're safe!'

'Well done, boy!' Sapt shouted. 'He believed you!'

Fritz stood up. He looked at me, up and down, down and up. Then he took a step backwards. 'Where's the King?' he cried.

'Be quiet,' Sapt warned him. 'Someone will hear!'

Fritz's face was white now. 'Is the King dead?' he asked quietly.

'Maybe not,' I answered. 'But he is Black Michael's prisoner.'

* * *

That day was a long one for me. Sapt talked to me for three hours about what I must do and what I must say, what I liked and what I didn't like. Then I had to do some of the King's business, but, because my finger was hurt, I did not have to write my name on any papers.

When, at last, I was alone with Sapt and Fritz, we started to talk about Black Michael. Fritz told me that Black Michael had six very dangerous men among his servants – three Ruritanians, a Belgian, a Frenchman and an Englishman. They did anything that the Duke ordered, and did not stop at murder. Three of them – the foreigners, Fritz had heard – were in Strelsau now with Duke Michael.

Sapt banged the table with his hand in excitement. 'Then the King must be alive! Michael's brought the

Majesty a word when speaking to a king (*Your Majesty*), or about a king (*His Majesty*)

murder the crime of killing someone

foreigner a person who comes from a different country

bang to make a loud noise

foreigners with him and left the three Ruritanians to hold the King prisoner. Usually the Six, as they're called, go everywhere with him.'

Fritz wanted to do something immediately about Black Michael and his men, but Sapt and I knew that we could not do anything openly.

'We'll play a waiting game and let Michael make the first move,' I said.

And so I stayed as King of Ruritania. In order to help the real King, I tried to make myself popular with the people. I went riding through the streets, smiling and talking to everybody.

Of course, I made many mistakes in my new life as King. But I talked my way out of them, with luck and with help from Fritz and Sapt. One time I met my brother Michael. We smiled and talked politely, but I could see the anger in his black eyes.

Chapter 6 **An adventure with a tea table**

O
ne day Sapt brought me some news – he had found out where the King was. Duke Michael was holding him prisoner somewhere in the Castle of Zenda.

Sapt also brought me a letter. It was in a woman's handwriting.

'I have an important message for you,' the letter began. 'Meet me tonight in the garden of the big house in New Avenue. Come at midnight, and come alone.'

There was another note on the back of the letter. 'Ask yourself which woman does not want Black Michael to marry Princess Flavia. From A. de M.'

'Antoinette de Mauban!' I cried. '*She* wants to marry the Duke, but he loves Princess Flavia.'

'That's true,' Sapt said. 'But you won't go, of course. They'll kill you! Duke Michael made her write this letter!'

'I must,' I replied. 'Every day we play this game there's more danger. I could make a mistake at any time, and if I do, we'll all die. Don't you see? I have to go tonight. We can't go on much longer.'

'Then I'm coming too,' said Sapt.

So, at half-past eleven that night, Sapt and I rode out to the house in New Avenue. We left Fritz to watch my room in the palace. The night was dark, so I took a lamp. I also had my revolver and a knife.

We soon reached the house and came to a gate in the wall. I got off my horse.

'I'll wait here,' said Sapt. 'If I hear anything, I'll …'

'Stay where you are!' I answered quickly. 'It's the King's only chance. They mustn't kill you too!'

handwriting the way someone writes

message something that one person tells another person to say to someone

marry to make someone your husband or wife

revolver a small gun, held in the hand

24

'You're right,' said Sapt. 'Good luck!'

Silently, I opened the gate and went into the garden. In front of me I could see the shape of a summer house and I moved towards it. Without a sound, I went up the steps, pushed open the door and went in. A woman hurried over to me.

summer house a small house in the garden

'Close the door!' she said. 'We must be quick, Mr Rassendyll! Michael made me write the letter — three men are coming to kill you — three of the Six! They'll tell everyone that Sapt and Fritz von Tarlenheim murdered you. Then Michael will make himself King and marry Princess Flavia.'

'But the King,' I said. 'I know he's in the Castle of Zenda, but where?'

'Go across the drawbridge and you will come to a heavy door . . . Listen! What's that? They're coming! They're too soon! Put out your lamp!' she cried, her eyes filled with fear. 'Quickly! You must go. There's a ladder at the end of the garden, next to the wall!'

But it was too late. The three men were already outside. There was a small hole in the door, and I put my eye to it. My hand was on my revolver. It was no good! There were three of them. I could kill one perhaps, but then . . .

A voice came from outside. 'Mr Rassendyll ...' It was the

Englishman. 'We only want to talk to you. Open the door.'

'We can talk through the door,' I replied. I looked through the hole again and saw that they were on the top step. When I opened the door, they would run at me.

'We'll let you go if you leave the country and we'll give you fifty thousand English pounds,' continued Detchard, the Englishman.

'Give me a minute to think,' I answered.

Wildly, I looked around the summer house and saw a metal garden table and some chairs. I picked up the table and held it in front of me, by the legs. Then I went to the back of the room and waited.

'All right, I agree,' I called. 'Open the door!'

I heard them arguing with each other, and then Detchard said to the Belgian, 'Why, Bersonin, are you scared of one man?'

A second later the door opened.

De Gautet, the Frenchman, was with the other two, and the three men were standing there with their revolvers ready. With a shout, I ran at them as hard as I could. They tried to shoot me, but the bullets hit the table. The next second the table knocked them to the ground and we all fell on top of each other. Quickly I picked myself up and ran for my life through the trees. I could hear them coming after me. Was Antoinette right? Was there really a ladder by the wall? I reached the end of the garden. The ladder was there! In a minute I was up it and over the wall.

Sapt was waiting with the horses and seconds later we were on our way home. And, as we rode, we laughed because I had fought Duke Michael's dangerous men — with a tea table!

shoot to hit with a gun

bullet a small piece of metal that comes out of a gun

Activities

1 Choose the best answer.

1 Why did Sapt tell Rudolf to go back to Strelsau?

a to help the real King ✓

b to help Duke Michael ☐

2 Where did they go after the fight with the Duke's men?

a the Castle of Zenda ☐

b Strelsau ☐

3 Who were the Six?

a Michael's servants ☐

b foreigners ☐

4 How did the table help to save Rudolf's life?

a The table fell on top of him. ☐

b The bullets hit the table. ☐

5 What did Rudolf use to escape from the garden?

a a ladder ☐

b a revolver ☐

2 Put these sentences in the correct order.

a They rode hard all night and reached Strelsau in the morning. ☐

b Sapt brought Rudolf a letter in a woman's handwriting. ☐

c They tried to shoot Rudolf but the bullets hit the table. ☐

d Rudolf made many mistakes in his new life as King. ☐

e Rudolf met Antoinette de Mauban in a summer house. ☐

f The men promised to give Rudolf fifty thousand pounds if he left the country. ☐

g Rudolf and Sapt killed three of Black Michael's men. 1

3 What did they say? Complete the sentences.

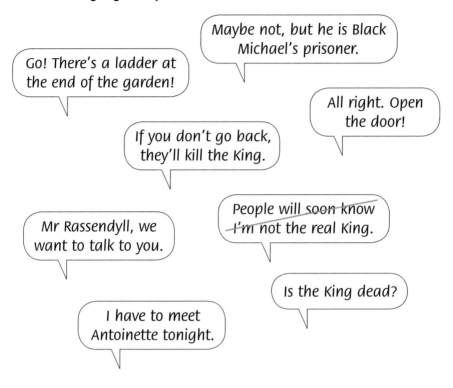

Maybe not, but he is Black Michael's prisoner.

Go! There's a ladder at the end of the garden!

All right. Open the door!

If you don't go back, they'll kill the King.

People will soon know I'm not the real King.

Mr Rassendyll, we want to talk to you.

Is the King dead?

I have to meet Antoinette tonight.

1 Rudolf said to Sapt, *'People will soon know I'm not the real King.'*

2 Sapt said to Rudolf _____

3 _____ Fritz asked.

4 _____ answered Rudolf.

5 _____ said Rudolf, reading the letter.

6 _____ cried Antoinette de Mauban.

7 Detchard, the Englishman said, _____

8 _____ said Rudolf.

Chapter 7 **Back to Zenda**

Every day I was sent a secret report by the Chief of Police, and the next afternoon I was playing cards with Fritz when Sapt brought it in. We learned that Duke Michael and the Three had left Strelsau, and that Antoinette de Mauban had also left. They had gone to Zenda.

'Sapt, we must also go to Zenda and bring the King home at once!' I cried.

And so the next day Sapt, Fritz and I left Strelsau to go to Tarlenheim House. This fine modern house belonged to Fritz's uncle and was near the Castle of Zenda. We had ten brave young men with us. Sapt had told them that a friend of the King's was a prisoner in the Castle of Zenda and that the King needed their help.

Michael, of course, knew of my arrival. I had not been in the house an hour when he sent three of the Six to me. These were not the three men who had tried to kill me. This time he sent the three Ruritanians – Lauengram, Krafstein and young Rupert of Hentzau.

'Duke Michael is very sorry that he can't welcome you himself,' explained Rupert of Hentzau. 'But, sadly, he's ill at the moment.'

'I hope that my dear brother will soon be better,' I replied with a smile.

Rupert threw back his head, shook his black hair and laughed.

'Oh, I'm sure he will!' he answered.

* * *

For dinner that evening, Fritz and I went to the little hotel in the town of Zenda where I had stayed before.

'Ask for a room where we can eat alone,' I said to Fritz. 'And ask the girl to bring our food.'

I covered my face and the girl came and put the food down on the table. When she turned to go, she looked at me and I let her see my face.

'The King!' she cried. 'You were the King! Oh, I'm sorry, sir! I'm sorry! The things that we said!'

'Forget that now,' I answered. 'You can help me. Tell no one that the King is here.'

She looked very serious.

'How's your friend Johann?' I began.

She looked surprised. 'Oh, we don't see him very often now,' she answered. 'He's very busy at the castle.'

'But could you ask Johann to come here tomorrow night? At ten o'clock, maybe, on the road out of Zenda.'

'Yes, sir ... You're not going to hurt him?'

'Not if he does what I say. Go now, and say nothing about this.'

After dinner, we left to go back to Tarlenheim House. We had almost reached it when we saw Sapt running to meet us.

'Have you seen them?' he cried.

'Who?' I asked.

'Duke Michael's men. Don't go out unless you have six men or more with you!' he said. 'You know Bernenstein, one of your men?'

'Of course,' I answered. 'A good, strong man, about as tall as me.'

'Well, they tried to kill him. He's upstairs now with a bullet in his arm. He was walking in the woods and he saw three men. Suddenly they started shooting at him, so he ran. He was lucky. They were scared to come too near the house, so he escaped. But it was you they wanted to kill!'

'Sapt,' I said, 'I'll do one thing for Ruritania before I leave it.'

'What's that?' asked Sapt.

'I'll kill every one of the Six. Ruritania will be a better place without them!'

CHAPTER 8 **News of the prisoner**

The next morning I was sitting in the garden in the sun when suddenly I saw young Rupert of Hentzau on horseback coming through the trees towards me. He was not scared of my men, but asked to speak with me alone. He said he had a message for me from the Duke of Strelsau. I asked my friends to move away, and Rupert came and sat down near me.

'Rassendyll,' he began, 'the Duke ...'

'Don't you know how to speak to the King?' I asked.

'Why pretend with me?'

'Because it isn't finished yet.'

'Well, I'm here because I want to help you ...'

'Then give me the message. What does the Duke want?' I asked.

'He wants you to leave. He'll take you safely out of the country and give you a hundred thousand pounds.'

'I refuse,' I replied immediately.

Rupert laughed. 'I knew it!' he cried. 'Duke Michael doesn't understand men like us! ... You must die then,' he added carelessly.

'Yes,' I answered. 'But you won't be alive to see me die!' I laughed. 'How's your prisoner?' I added.

'Alive,' he replied. 'But for how long, who knows?' And he laughed loudly.

I took a step towards him. 'Go now, before I kill you,' I shouted angrily.

Rupert turned, but suddenly he came back. He put out his right hand. 'Shake hands!' he called.

Of course, he knew what I would do. I put my hands behind my back. Quickly, his left hand moved towards me. In it, he held a dagger and it was coming straight at my heart! I jumped to one side, and the dagger went deep into my shoulder.

Before my friends could do anything, Rupert of Hentzau was on his horse and galloping through the trees. I heard my men going after him with their guns – and then everything went black.

When I awoke it was dark, and Fritz was at my bedside. He told me that I was not badly hurt, and that the plan to catch Johann had been successful.

'He seems pleased to be here,' Fritz said. 'I think he's scared of Duke Michael.'

Later Sapt brought Johann up to see me. At first Johann was scared to speak, but then he started to talk. We asked him many questions, and finally Johann gave us the information we wanted.

In the Castle of Zenda, near the drawbridge and below the ground, there were two small rooms, cut out of the rock. In the first of these rooms there were always three of the Six. At the back of this room there was a door which went into the second room. The King was in the second room.

'If someone tries to get into the first room, two of the three men will fight, but Rupert of Hentzau or Detchard will run into the second room and kill the King,' Johann said. 'There's a small window in the second room with a large pipe going down into the moat outside,' he went on. 'You can get a man inside it, and they'll tie a heavy stone to the King's body and push it down the pipe. The body will go down and disappear under the water, and

dagger a sharp knife used for fighting

shoulder the top of the arm where it joins the body

successful getting or doing what you want

information things that you want to know about something, facts

pipe a round piece of metal, used for transporting things like water

disappear to go away suddenly

35

the murderers will then go down the pipe themselves, and swim across the moat.'

'And if I bring an army to the castle?' I asked.

'Duke Michael will still murder the King,' replied Johann. 'He won't fight. He'll kill the King and push his body down the pipe. And he'll put one of the Six in the prison. He'll say the man had done something to make him angry. That will stop the stories about a prisoner in Zenda.' Johann stopped for a minute, but then he added, 'If they know I've told you this, they'll kill me. They're all bad, but Rupert of Hentzau is the worst. Don't let them kill me ...'

'All right,' I said. 'But if anyone asks you who the prisoner of Zenda is, don't tell him. If you do, I'll kill you myself!'

Johann left the room and I looked at Sapt.

'It doesn't matter what plan we make,' I said. 'The King will be dead before we can get to him!'

Sapt shook his grey head angrily. 'You'll still be King of Ruritania in a year's time.'

'Maybe one of the Duke's men will turn against him ...' I said.

'Impossible,' replied Sapt.

'Then I don't know what we'll do,' I said.

Activities

1 Are these sentences true (T) or false (F)?

1 Black Michael sent Rupert of Hentzau to see Rudolf. `T`

2 Black Michael's men tried to kill Johann. ☐

3 The Duke wanted Rudolf to leave Ruritania. ☐

4 Rupert of Hentzau tried to break Rudolf's arm. ☐

5 The King was being held prisoner in the Castle of Zenda. ☐

6 One of the Six was the prisoner of Zenda. ☐

2 Complete the sentences with these words.

> shoulder   bullet   ~~alone~~   dagger   pipe   message

1 'Ask for a room where we can eat _____*alone*_____.'

2 'Bernenstein is upstairs now with a _____ in his arm.'

3 Rupert said he had a _____ for Rudolf from the Duke of Strelsau.

4 Rupert's hand held a _____ .

5 It went deep into Rudolf's _____ .

6 'There's a large _____ going down into the moat outside.'

3 **Correct the mistakes in the story.**

the Chief of Police

Rudolf, Fritz and Sapt learn from ~~Antoinette de Mauban~~ that Duke Michael and

the Three have left Strelsau. So they go to a hotel near the Castle of Zenda. Four

brave young men go with them. Michael sends three of the Six to see Rudolf.

Rupert of Hentzau tells Rudolf that the Duke hasn't come himself because he

is busy. That evening Fritz and Sapt go to have dinner in the hotel where Rudolf

stayed before. After dinner Sapt tells Rupert not to go out alone. He says Duke

Michael's men started smiling at Bernenstein. The next day Rupert tries to hit

Rudolf.

4 **What do you think happens next? Tick the boxes.**

	Yes	No
1 Johann tells their plan to Duke Michael.	☐	☐
2 Rudolf swims in the moat.	☐	☐
3 Rudolf and his men kill two of the Six.	☐	☐
4 Rupert tries to shoot the King.	☐	☐
5 Rudolf makes friends with Duke Michael.	☐	☐
6 Antoinette de Mauban asks Rudolf for help.	☐	☐

Chapter 9 **A night outside the castle**

pretend to try to
make somebody
believe something

rope thick, strong
string; you can
pull things with it

I wanted Duke Michael to think that I was still very ill, so we told the newspapers that the King had had a very serious accident.

We had sent Johann back to the Castle of Zenda and suddenly we had a message from him. The real King was very ill.

'We must save him,' I said to Sapt. I added quickly, 'I can't go on pretending like this much longer.'

So Sapt and I made our plans.

* * *

Late the next night, Sapt, Fritz and I, with six more men, rode out towards the Castle of Zenda. Sapt was carrying a long rope and I had a short, thick stick and a long knife.

The night was dark, and it was wet and windy. We stayed away from the town and we met no one. When we came to the moat, we stopped near some trees and the

six men hid there with the horses. Then Sapt tied the rope around one of the trees near the water. I pulled off my boots, put the stick between my teeth and gently went down the rope into the water. I was going to take a look at the pipe.

It had been warm and bright that day, and the water was not cold. Slowly and carefully I swam around the dark walls of the castle. There were lights in the new buildings, and from time to time I heard people shouting and laughing. 'That must be young Rupert and his friends,' I thought. Suddenly a dark shape appeared in front of me. It was the pipe! The bottom of it was very wide and came out into the moat. And then I saw something which nearly made my heart stop. It was a boat, and in the boat there was a man! His gun was beside him, but, luckily, he was asleep. As quietly as I could, I moved closer. The man still slept.

I had very little time. Someone could come at any minute. I looked up at where the pipe went through the wall into the prison. There was a thin line of light at the bottom edge. I heard Detchard's voice, and then I heard the King reply. Just then the light went out, and, in the darkness, I heard the King crying. I did not call to him. I had to get away safely – and take the watchman with me.

I climbed quietly into the boat and hit the man hard on the head with my stick. He fell back in the boat without a sound. No one could hear me because the wind was strong. But from somewhere behind me, I heard a shout. Someone was calling to the watchman. I reached the side of the moat where Sapt and Fritz were waiting. Quickly, I tied the rope round the man's body and Sapt and Fritz pulled it up. Then I climbed up the rope myself.

'Call our men from the trees,' I said quietly. 'And hurry!'

But just then, three men rode round from the front of the castle. Luckily, they did not see us, but they heard our six friends riding out of the trees, and with a shout they galloped towards them.

Seconds later we heard the sound of shots, and I ran to help our men. Sapt and Fritz followed.

'Kill them!' cried a voice. It was Rupert of Hentzau.

'Too late! They've got both of us!' cried another voice. 'Save yourself, Rupert!'

I ran on, holding my stick in my hand. Suddenly, through the darkness, I saw a horse coming towards me. I jumped at the horse's head, and saw the man's face above me.

'At last!' I shouted. 'Rupert of Hentzau!'

He had only his sword, and my men were coming at him from one side, and Sapt and Fritz from the other.

Rupert laughed. 'It's the play-actor!' he cried, and with this sword he hit my stick from my hand. Then he turned

his horse, galloped to the moat and jumped into the water with our bullets flying round our ears. Our men tried to shoot him in the water, but it was too dark and we lost him.

We had killed two of the Six – Lauengram and Krafstein – but I was angry. Three of our brave friends were also dead, and we carried them home with a heavy heart.

And I did not like to hear Rupert call me a play-actor.

*　*　*

Of course, Michael and I could not let the people know that we were enemies. So, in the daytime it was safe to be in the town of Zenda. One day, soon after our night outside the castle, I was riding through the town when I saw a group of people dressed in black. Rupert of Hentzau was with them, and when he saw me he turned his horse and came towards me.

'It's the funeral of my dear friend, Lauengram,' he said, in answer to our question.

'I'm sorry your friend is dead,' I said to him.

Rupert turned and rode away. I went after him.

'You fought bravely the other night,' I said, 'and you're young. Help me save the King – and I'll help you.'

But Rupert was not interested. 'No,' he answered. 'But if they were both dead – the King and the Duke – then you could be King, and I could be rich.'

When I returned home, there was a message from Antoinette de Mauban.

'I helped you once. Help me now. Save me from this terrible place! Save me from these murderers!'

I was sorry for her, but what could I do?

funeral the time when a dead person is put under the ground

Chapter 10 **A dangerous plan**

One day Johann came to tell us that the King was now very sick, and that Antoinette de Mauban and a doctor were looking after him.

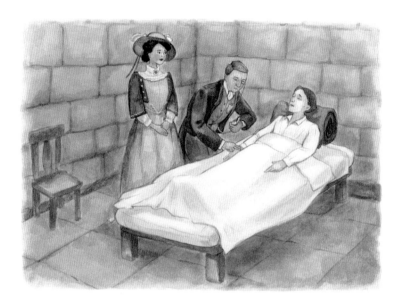

Two of the Six were now dead, but there were always two men watching the King. The other two slept in a room above and would hear them if they called. Detchard and Bersonin watched by night; Rupert of Hentzau and De Gautet by day. The Duke's rooms were on the first floor, in the new buildings of the castle, and Antoinette's room was on the same floor. But at night the Duke locked the door of her room, and pulled up the drawbridge. He kept the key himself. Johann slept near the front door of the new castle with five other men – but they had no guns.

We could not wait any longer. 'Listen!' I said to Johann. 'I'll make you rich if you do what I say.' Johann agreed.

sick not feeling well, ill

'You must take this letter to Madame de Mauban,' I said, 'and tomorrow, at two o'clock in the morning, you must open the front door of the new castle. Tell the others that you need air, or something – and then escape.'

Johann was very scared, but he seemed to understand. I explained my plan to Sapt and Fritz.

'When Johann opens the front door,' I said, 'Sapt and his men will run into the castle and hold the men who are sleeping there. At the same time Antoinette will scream loudly again and again. She'll cry "Help! Help me, Michael!" And she'll shout Rupert of Hentzau's name. Duke Michael will hear and he'll run out of this room – straight into the hands of Sapt! Sapt will get the key from the Duke and let down the drawbridge. Rupert and De Gautet will hear the noise and hurry to cross the drawbridge. I'll hide by the bridge, in the moat, and when they try to cross, I'll kill them. Then we'll hurry to the room in the old castle where the King is, and kill Detchard and Bersonin before they have time to kill the King.'

The others listened in silence. It was a very dangerous plan, and I did not really think it would work – but we had to try!

Activities

1 Match the two halves of the sentences.

1 Rudolf swam around the castle to find the pipe . . . [b]

a telling her to scream for Duke Michael's help in the night.

2 Rudolf and his friends killed two of the Six that night, . . . ☐

b which went from the prisoner's room down into the moat.

3 The plan was for Johann to take a letter to Antoinette, . . . ☐

c and then enter the old castle and save the King.

4 Johann would open the front door . . . ☐

d but they also lost three of their own men.

5 Rudolf would hide in the moat by the drawbridge, . . . ☐

e in order to let Sapt and his men into the new castle.

2 Complete the sentences with these words.

murderers   ~~accident~~   drawbridge   funeral   scared   floor

watchman

1 Rudolf told the newspapers that the King had had a very serious
   ___accident___ .

2 Rudolf saw that a _____ was asleep in the boat.

3 Rupert of Hentzau was dressed in black for his friend's _____ .

4 Antoinette wrote: 'Save me from these _____ !'

5 The Duke's rooms were on the first _____ .

6 At night the Duke pulled up the _____ .

7 Johann was _____ when he heard Rudolf's plan.

3 Find words in the word snake to complete the sentences.

crossbraverichwallssickmoatplanplace

1 Slowly and carefully I swam around the ___walls___ of the castle.

2 I reached the side of the _____ where Sapt and Fritz were waiting.

3 Three of our _____ friends were dead.

4 'Save me from this terrible _____!'

5 Johann came to tell us that the King was now very _____.

6 'I'll make you _____ if you do what I say,' Rudolf told Johann.

7 'When they try to _____ the drawbridge, I'll kill them.'

8 It was a very dangerous _____, but we had to try!

4 Correct the underlined words in these sentences.

1 Rudolf didn't want to present he was the King any more. ___pretend___

2 Rudolf went down a ripe into the water. _____

3 Rudolf heard the King lying. _____

4 Rupert hit Rudolf's stick with his sworn. _____

5 Rudolf's men tried to shout Rupert in the water. _____

6 Rudolf asked Rupert to help him same the King. _____

Chapter 11 **The prisoner and the King**

We needed bad weather, but it was a fine, clear night. At midnight Sapt, Fritz and their men left and rode quietly through the woods towards the castle. If everything went well, they would get there at a quarter to two and wait for Johann to open the front door. If Johann did not open the door, Fritz would come round to the other side of the castle to find me. If I was not there, then I was dead – and the King, too! Sapt and his men would go back to Tarlenheim House and return with the Marshal and more men to get into the castle.

So, half an hour later, I too left Tarlenheim. I took a shorter way than Sapt, and when I reached the moat I hid my horse in the trees, tied my rope round a strong tree and let myself down into the water. Slowly, I began to swim along under the castle walls. Just after a quarter to one, I came to the pipe and waited quietly in its shadow. Light was coming from Duke Michael's window opposite me across the moat, and I could see into the room. The next window along, which Johann had said was Antoinette's room, was dark.

Then the Duke's window opened, and Antoinette de Mauban looked out. Behind her there was a man. Rupert of Hentzau! What was he doing in the Duke's room? I wondered.

At that moment I heard the door of the room open and then the angry voice of Duke Michael.

'What are you doing here?' he cried.

'Waiting for you, sir,' Rupert replied quickly.

'Well, now you can go to bed. Are Detchard and Bersonin watching the prisoner?'

'Yes, sir.'

A few minutes later Rupert crossed the drawbridge and it was pulled up. The light in Duke Michael's room went out, but a light came on, and stayed on, in Antoinette's room. In the silent darkness, I waited.

For about ten minutes everything was quiet, but suddenly I heard a noise on my side of the moat. A dark shape appeared in the gateway to the bridge, then turned and began to climb down some hidden steps in the wall. It was Rupert of Hentzau again – with a sword! Silently he went down into the water and swam across the moat. Then he climbed out and I heard him unlock the door. It was clear that Rupert of Hentzau had his own secret plans for that night.

gateway
entrance

It was not yet time for Johann to open the front door for my friends, and I still had to wait. I climbed up to the gateway of the bridge and hid in a dark corner. Now no one could enter or leave the old castle without fighting me. I wondered what Rupert was doing now, and a few seconds later I found out.

There was a sudden crash, and then a woman's screams rang through the night.

'Help me, Michael! Rupert of Hentzau!'

Those were the words that I had written for Antoinette! But these were screams of real fear and soon I heard shouts and the sound of fighting from Antoinette's room. Then Rupert appeared at the window. His back was towards me, but he was fighting. 'That's for you, Johann,' I heard him cry. Then, 'Come on, Michael!'

So Johann was in there too, fighting at the Duke's side! How could he open the door for Sapt now?

More of the Duke's men had run to the room and the noise of the fighting grew louder. Suddenly Rupert gave a wild laugh, and with his sword in his hand, jumped from the window into the moat below.

At that moment the door of the old castle opened and De Gautet appeared beside me. I jumped at him with my sword, and a second later he fell dead in the doorway without a word or a sound.

Wildly, I searched his body for the keys. I found them, and in a minute I was in the first room, where Bersonin and Detchard were. But there was only Bersonin in the room. Before he had time to realize that I was there, I had killed him. Detchard had run into the King's room and locked the door behind him. I ran at it to break it down. But would I be in time? Was the King already dead?

The King was standing helplessly by the wall. But the doctor was also in the room and the brave little man had thrown himself at Detchard. He gave his life for the King, because, as I entered, Detchard pulled himself free and drove his sword into the doctor's side. Then, with an angry shout, Detchard turned to me.

We fought long and hard. Detchard was an excellent swordsman, and I was growing tired. He drove me back against the wall, gave me a deep cut in the arm, and began to smile. In a second he would kill me.

Suddenly, the King realized who I was.

'Cousin Rudolf!' he cried. Then he picked up a chair and threw it at Detchard's legs. The Englishman, jumping to one side, turned his sword against the King, and with a cry the King fell to the ground. Detchard moved towards me again, stepped in the doctor's blood on the floor – and fell to the ground himself. I had him! A second later his body lay across the dead doctor.

But was the King dead? I had no time to find out, because just then I heard the noise of the drawbridge coming down. And Rupert of Hentzau was still alive. The King must wait for help while I fought his enemies.

I ran out of the room and up the steps towards the drawbridge. And then I heard the sound of laughter – Rupert of Hentzau was laughing!

He was standing alone in the middle of the bridge. In the gateway on the far side stood a group of the Duke's men. They seemed too frightened to move.

'Come out, Michael, you dog!' Rupert shouted.

But a woman's wild cry answered him. 'He's dead! He's dead!'

The men in the gateway moved to one side and a woman came forward. Her face was as white as her long dress, and her dark hair lay over her shoulders. In her hand she held a gun.

The shot rang out, but she missed. Rupert laughed. Again Antoinette de Mauban faced him, her gun ready. But before she could shoot, Rupert jumped over the side of the bridge, and down into the moat below.

At that moment I heard the sound of running feet inside the new castle – and the welcome voice of my old friend, Captain Sapt! Then I knew that the King was safe and needed me no more. I ran out on to the bridge and jumped down into the moat. I had a fight to finish with Rupert of Hentzau.

miss to not hit

*   *   *

I swam hard and caught up with him round the corner of the old castle. He had found my rope, climbed out of the moat, and was already running towards the trees where I had left my horse.

I ran after him as fast as I could. He turned and saw me, and called out, laughing, 'Why, it's the play-actor!' But then, with a cry of surprise, he found my horse, and in a minute he was on its back.

'Get down!' I shouted. 'Stand and fight, like a man!'

He turned, waiting for me, and I ran at him with my sword. For a few minutes we fought wildly. Blood ran from his face where I had cut it, but I had fought too many fights that night. He would surely kill me now.

I was saved by Fritz, who came galloping around the castle to find me. When Rupert saw him coming, he knew he had no chance.

'Goodbye, Rudolf Rassendyll!' he called. 'We'll meet again!'

And he rode away into the forest, laughing and singing … and still alive.

I fell to the ground. Blood was running again from the cut in my arm, and I could not stand. Fritz jumped down from his horse and helped me.

'Dear friend!' he said. 'Thank goodness I've found you! When Johann did not come, we had to break down the castle door. We were afraid we would be too late.'

'And the King …?' I said.

'Because of a very brave Englishman,' Fritz said gently, 'the King is alive.'

Chapter 12 **Goodbye to Ruritania**

Old Sapt worked hard to keep our secret hidden. He sent messages, told lies and gave orders. All his plans were successful – no one ever found out that for a short while there were two Kings in Ruritania.

Before I returned to England, I saw the King once more. He thanked me and shook my hand. We both knew that we would never meet again – it was too dangerous, and I knew then that I didn't want any more adventures.

*   *   *

I live quietly now, but every year Fritz and I meet in a little town outside Ruritania. There, he gives me news of the King and his wife, Queen Flavia. And every year I think about how I too was once King Rudolf of Ruritania!

Activities

1 Correct the mistakes in these sentences.

Rupert of Hentzau

1 When Antoinette screamed, ~~no one~~ was in her room.

2 Sapt and Fritz could not get in through the castle door because Johann was

fighting on the drawbridge.

3 Duke Michael killed Antoinette, so Rupert of Hentzau tried to shoot the Duke.

4 Rudolf killed the other four of the Six.

5 Rudolf and Rupert fought wildly, and Rupert was killed.

6 The people of Ruritania found out who Rudolf really was.

2 Find fifteen words from the story in this word square.

h	d	a	g	g	e	r	e	d	l	l
k	p	s	w	i	m	r	m	r	c	a
n	c	e	m	i	c	o	h	a	o	d
i	a	m	o	a	t	p	a	w	h	d
f	s	e	l	r	u	e	p	b	o	e
e	t	l	e	t	t	e	r	r	t	r
t	l	b	u	l	l	e	t	i	e	k
h	e	e	s	w	o	r	d	d	l	i
r	e	v	o	l	v	e	r	g	t	n
z	a	p	r	i	s	o	n	e	r	g

3   **Who do these sentences describe? Write the names.**

Duke Michael   Antoinette de Mauban   Rudolf Rassendyll

Rupert of Hentzau

1   _Rupert of Hentzau_   was a young Ruritanian nobleman.

2   _____ was a beautiful French lady.

3   _____ was a young English nobleman.

4   _____ was the King's half-brother.

5   _____ had the Elphberg hair and nose.

6   _____ was a wild and dangerous fighter.

7   _____ loved Duke Michael.

8   _____ wanted to be the King and to marry Flavia.

9   _____ tried to kill Rudolf Rassendyll several times.

10 _____ looked just like the King.

11 _____ kept the King a prisoner in the Castle of Zenda.

12 _____ was one of Duke Michael's men.

13 _____ agreed to take the King's place.

14 _____ planned to kill the King if anyone tried to
    rescue him.

15 _____ tried to help Rudolf Rassendyll rescue the King.

16 _____ wanted the chance of a great adventure.

Project

1 Imagine you are going to be the king or queen of a new country.

1 What are you going to wear? Tick the boxes and add your own ideas.

☐ a crown   ☐ jewels   ☐ a cloak   ☐ expensive clothes

2 How are you going to travel?

☐ car   ☐ carriage   ☐ helicopter   ☐ horse

3 Write down three things you are going to do as king or queen.

4 Design a flag for your country. What is your country called? _____

2 Now imagine all the things you have done in one day as king or queen and write a diary. Fill in the gaps.

Dear Diary,

Today I got up at _____ . After breakfast I

I wore my _____ . We saw

went to _____ . Then I came back to

_____ .

the palace. I rode in the royal _____ .

At the palace I had to see _____

Then I had half an hour free so I decided to _____ . Then it was

_____ . At two

lunchtime. I ate _____ . Then

o'clock I went to see _____

when I came back I had a rest until _____

o'clock. At six o'clock I welcomed the king and queen of

_____ who were visiting our country.

For the royal dinner we ate _____ .

Tomorrow I am going to _____

_____ .

OXFORD

UNIVERSITY PRESS

Great Clarendon Street, Oxford OX2 6DP

Oxford University Press is a department of the University of Oxford.
It furthers the University's objective of excellence in research, scholarship,
and education by publishing worldwide in

Oxford New York

Auckland Cape Town Dar es Salaam Hong Kong Karachi
Kuala Lumpur Madrid Melbourne Mexico City Nairobi
New Delhi Shanghai Taipei Toronto

With offices in

Argentina Austria Brazil Chile Czech Republic France Greece
Guatemala Hungary Italy Japan Poland Portugal Singapore
South Korea Switzerland Thailand Turkey Ukraine Vietnam

OXFORD and OXFORD ENGLISH are registered trade marks of
Oxford University Press in the UK and in certain other countries

ISBN: 978 0 19 480299 4

Printed in China.

ACKNOWLEDGEMENTS

IIllustrations by: Katy Jackson/The Bright Agency